This b

_____

Published by Ladybird Books Ltd
A Penguin Company
Penguin Books Ltd, 80 Strand, London WC2R 0RL, UK
Penguin Books Australia Ltd, Camberwell, Victoria, Australia
Penguin Books (NZ) Ltd, 67 Apollo Drive, Rosedale, North Shore 0632, New Zealand

1 3 5 7 9 10 8 6 4 2

© LADYBIRD BOOKS MMVII

ISBN: 978-1-8464-6-541-3

Printed in Italy

Extreme Weather

written by Lorraine Horsley
illustrated by Laszlo Veres

Weather is the way the air around us changes.

It can be wet.

It can be dry.

It can be cold.

It can be hot.

In some places the weather is very dry.
In some places the weather is very wet.

Deserts are very dry places.

Clouds form when there is a lot of water in the air. Water falls from the clouds as rain.

Too much rain can cause floods and landslides.

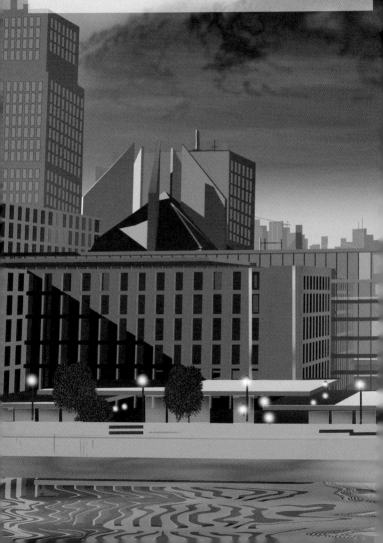

Storm clouds form when the air is hot and wet.

Electricity in storm clouds causes lightning.

Sometimes storm clouds form over warm oceans. When the wind in these storms reaches 119 kilometres per hour, it is called a hurricane.

When hurricanes reach land they can cause a lot of damage.

In some places the weather
is very hot.
In some places the weather
is very cold.

Antarctica is a very cold place.

Sometimes when the air is very cold, the water in storm clouds falls as blocks of ice. These are called hailstones.

A hailstone that fell in Nebraska, USA, was as big as a football.

Sometimes when the air is very cold, the water in clouds falls as snow.

When the wind blows the snow
it can cause a blizzard.

In some places the weather is very calm. In some places the weather is very windy.

calm

breeze

near gale

strong gale

The fastest winds are tornadoes. The winds in a tornado can reach 480 kilometres per hour.

Tornadoes can lift people and cars into the air.

People can cause changes to the weather. Over time, gases from cars, rubbish dumps and burning fuel can cause the temperature to go up.

This is called global warming.

What is the weather like today where you live?

hot

rainy

windy

cold

cloudy

snowy

stormy

Index

blizzard	20–21
desert	8–9
floods	11
gale	23
global warming	27
hurricane	14–15
landslide	11
lightning	13
snow	20–21, 29
tornado	24–25